Favorite Action BIBLE VERSES

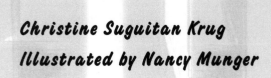

Christine Suguitan Krug

Illustrated by Nancy Munger

Finger Plays for God's Word

CONCORDIA PUBLISHING HOUSE • SAINT LOUIS

1 2 3 4 5 6 7 8 9 10   12 11 10 09 08 07 06 05 04 03

Contents

Hints for Parents and Teachers

Finger plays offer repetition, which creates life-long learning, and fun, which sparks interest and enthusiasm. Young children love them. And that makes these simple exercises very effective for teaching God's Word and the promise of salvation through the death and resurrection of Jesus Christ.

The finger plays in this book can be used with classroom or family devotions. They can be incorporated into story time. They can be used to help children memorize Bible verses. Or they can be used when children simply need a break or to fill an extra minute with meaningful activity. Take a moment to talk about the verses and their meaning for us, His children.

However you choose to use the finger plays in this collection, they are designed to help you and the children you work with share love for our Lord and witness to faith in His certain promises as revealed in the Scriptures.

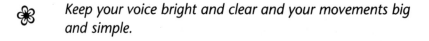

Keep your voice bright and clear and your movements big and simple.

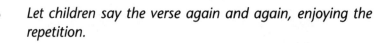

Let children say the verse again and again, enjoying the repetition.

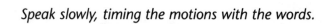

Speak slowly, timing the motions with the words.

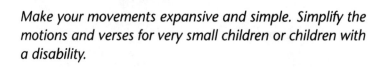

Make your movements expansive and simple. Simplify the motions and verses for very small children or children with a disability.

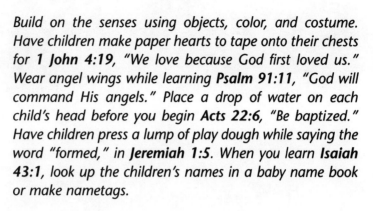

❀ *Build on the senses using objects, color, and costume. Have children make paper hearts to tape onto their chests for **1 John 4:19**, "We love because God first loved us." Wear angel wings while learning **Psalm 91:11**, "God will command His angels." Place a drop of water on each child's head before you begin **Acts 22:6**, "Be baptized." Have children press a lump of play dough while saying the word "formed," in **Jeremiah 1:5**. When you learn **Isaiah 43:1**, look up the children's names in a baby name book or make nametags.*

❀ *With tambourine or drum, let the children bang out the rhythm of verses as you recite them.*

❀ *Pick out hats for wearing, or designate a special corner or circle, just for performing the verses.*

❀ *Talk about the motions. When you enact **Psalm 28:7**, "My heart leaps for joy," the hands leap forward. Ask, what are our hands like? Maybe they're like dolphins, leaping from the water. Help the children picture things. Some of the imagined objects in this book are a clock, a rolling drum, and a baby.*

❀ *Say and do the verse with children as slowly as they can. Then try it as fast as they can.*

❀ *Say the verse quietly or shout it loud. You might start in whispers and gradually increase volume.*

❀ *Try this: let the children say the words in their minds, but not aloud, while they pantomime. Then add the words again.*

❀ *For older children, discuss why a particular action may have been chosen. For **1 John 2:12**, why does a frown stand for sins?*

❀ *When coloring reproduced pages, encourage children to say the verses. Display colored pages at school, home, or church as reminders.*

Genesis 1:10

God

(Point to God.)

saw that it was

*(Shield eyes with hand;
look left, middle, and right.)*

good.

(Clap hands in applause.)

Numbers 10:29

The Lord

(Point to God.)

has promised

(Raise one hand, palm out.)

good things.

(Bring hand to mouth, kiss fingertips.)

Psalm 16:1

❀

Keep

(Cup hands.)

me

(Point to self.)

safe,

(Close cupped hands and bring up to chin, as if protecting a small creature.)

O God.

(Point to God.)

9

Psalm 28:7

My

(Place hand on chest.)

heart

(Both hands over heart.)

leaps

*(Make hands leap forward
together.)*

for joy.

(Raise both hands high. Smile.)

11

Psalm 81:1

❀

Sing

(Sing the word "sing," one hand on chest, one hand out, like an opera singer.)

for joy

(Raise both hands. Smile.)

to God.

(Point to God.)

Psalm 86:6

Hear

(Cup ear with hand.)

my prayer,

(Fold hands in prayer.)

O Lord.

(Bow head over hands.)

Psalm 91:11

[God]

(Point to God.)

will command

(Clap hands once, with force.)

His angels . . .

(Hands up at shoulders.
With one hand, circle head.)

to guard

*(Hold elbows out,
and touch both fists together.)*

you

(Point to others.)

in all

(Spread arms wide.)

your ways.

*(Hands together, move them as if
going down winding roads.)*

Psalm 121:5

The LORD

(Point to God.)

watches

*(Shield eyes with hand,
looking left and right.)*

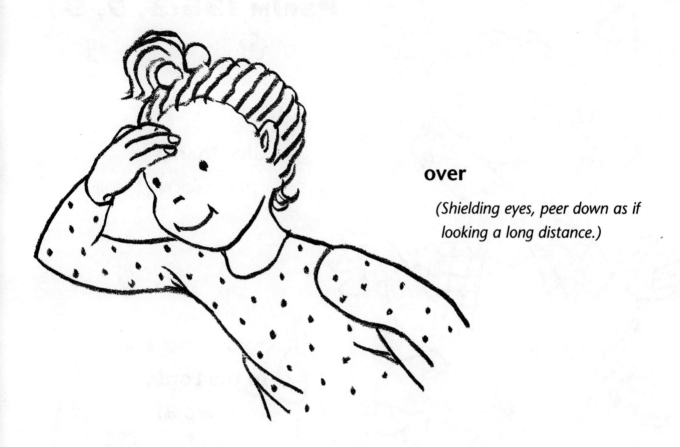

over

(Shielding eyes, peer down as if looking a long distance.)

you.

(Point to others.)

Psalm 136:3, 7, 9

Give thanks

(Hold hands out; look up.)

to the Lord . . .

(Point to God.)

who made . . .

*(Press palms together
as if molding clay.)*

the moon

(Make a circle with arms over head.)

and stars.

(Lift one hand. At different points in the air, rub thumb against fingertips for "twinkling" stars.)

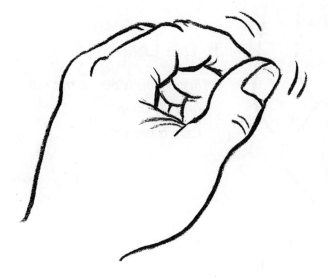

Psalm 145:3

Great

(Roll hands around each other to represent the sound of a drum roll.)

is the LORD!

(Bring hands out of the roll and lift them high. Give a big smile.)

Proverbs 17:17

A friend

*(Hook arm around the neck
of real or imagined friend.)*

loves

(Clasp hands over heart.)

at all times.

*(Draw a circle in the air, as if
moving the hands of a clock.)*

Isaiah 43:1

I

(Point to self.)

have called

(Hold a "phone" to your ear.)

you

(Point to others.)

by your name.

*(Brush forefinger on chest to
"read" an imaginary name tag.)*

Jeremiah 1:5

[God said . . .]

(Point to God.)

"Before I formed

(Cup and press hands together as if forming clay.)

you . . .

(Point to others.)

I knew

(Tap forehead.)

you."

(Point to others.)

25

Matthew 4:19

Come,

(Stretch arms forward in an inviting motion.)

follow Me.

(Motion for someone behind you to follow.)

Matthew 7:11

[God]

(Point to God.)

gives

(Stretch out both hands, palms up.)

good gifts.

(Make a circle with arms out in front of you. Stagger as if trying to manage an armload of gifts.)

Matthew 28:20

I

(Point to self.)

am with

(Hug self.)

you

(Point to others.)

always.

(Stretch arms wide to your sides.)

Mark 10:14

Let the little children

(Squat down, close to the ground.)

come

(While squatting, hold out hands in inviting gesture.)

to Me.

(Point to self.)

Luke 2:11

❀

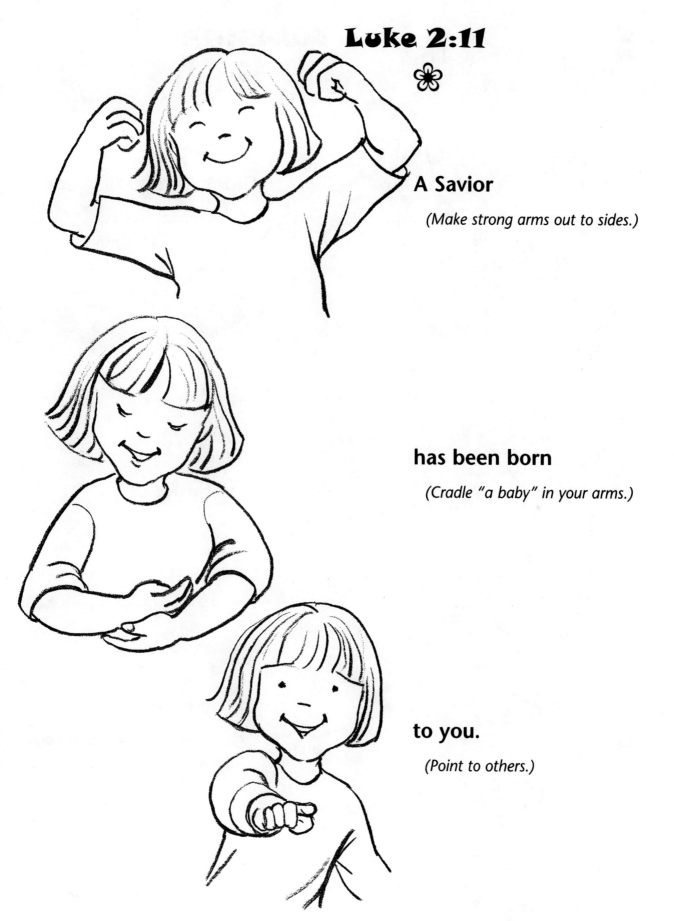

A Savior

(Make strong arms out to sides.)

has been born

(Cradle "a baby" in your arms.)

to you.

(Point to others.)

Luke 2:14

❀

Glory

(Lower hands from sky, wiggling fingers slowly.)

to God

(Point to God.)

in the highest.

(Standing on tiptoes, stretch arms as high as you can.)

Luke 11:4

Forgive

(Bow head. Touch forehead with clasped hands.)

us

(Place hand on chest.)

our sins.

(Frown and touch corners of mouth with fingertips.)

Acts 22:16

Be baptized

(Place both hands on head.)

and wash

(Rub your hands together, pretending to wash hands, shoulders, face.)

your sins

(Frown and touch fingers to the corners of your mouth.)

away.

(Move hands away from face while breaking into a smile.)

1 Corinthians 15:3

❀

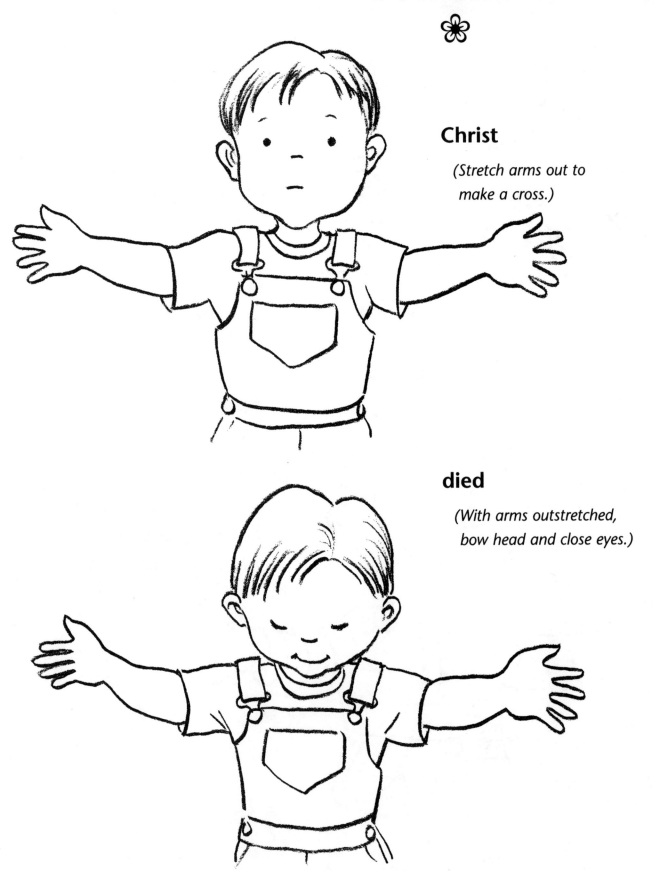

Christ

(Stretch arms out to make a cross.)

died

(With arms outstretched, bow head and close eyes.)

for our

(Place hand on chest.)

sins.

*(Frown and touch fingers
to the corners of your mouth.)*

Philippians 4:4

Rejoice

(Raise your hands and smile wide.)

in the Lord

(Point to God.)

always.

(Palms together in front of you, stretch arms further and further apart.)

I will say it again:

(Point to mouth, nodding.)

Rejoice!

(Raise your arms and jump up happily.)

1 Thessalonians 4:14

We

*(Point to self, others,
then self again.)*

believe

(Place hands over your heart.)

that Jesus died

(Stretch arms wide to make a cross with your body. Lean your head against shoulder, eyes closed.)

and rose again.

(Bring both hands high over head, as you open your eyes and smile.)

2 Timothy 1:3

I . . . remember

(Tap forehead with finger.)

you

(Point to others.)

in my prayers

(Fold hands in prayer.)

[night

(Lay folded hands against cheek and lean head to one side as if sleeping.)

and day.]

(Open eyes and look toward the sky.)

2 Timothy 3:14

❀

Continue

(Hands out in front of you, palms down. Make "steps" in the air.)

in what you

(Point to others.)

have learned.

(Point to head.)

1 John 2:12

Your

(Point to others.)

sins

(Look down, frown, touch corners of mouth with fingers.)

have been forgiven.

(Look up and smile, framing face with hands.)

1 John 3:2

Now

(Point to ground at feet.)

we are

*(Point to self, others,
then self again.)*

children

*(Place hand on head.
Crouch down to be smaller.)*

of God.

(Point to God.)

1 John 4:7

Love

(Hug self.)

comes from God.

(Wiggle fingers as hands move down from the sky, like rain.)

1 John 4:19

We

(Point to others, then self.)

love

(Hug self.)

because [God] first

(Strike forefinger against palm.)

loved us.

*(Give self a long hug,
rocking from side to side.)*